Images

---

by Alan Cooke

Still Water Publishing
PO Box 76
Copeville TX 75121-9998
www.alan-cooke.com

Book cover & design by Alan Cooke

The text in this book is set in Helvetica
Manufactured in the United States

ISBN: 9780985135003

Dedicated to all frustrated artists...

Contents

Black.....1
Joey's Boat.....3
Chicken Nuggets.....14
The Curse of the Poet.....15
Hammer vs. Radio.....16
Broken.....18
Teacher.....19
Poetastry.....21
2038.....23
Advice, take mine.....25
Anna.....27
Warning.....31
We.....32
If.....33
Teresa.....34
El Paso.....35
Imagine That.....37
Autumn.....38
Birthday toast.....39
This Mind.....40
Indian Blood.....42
So Strange.....43
Circle.....44
Silence.....45
Demons.....46
The Terrible Parable.....47
She Sang.....49
Dream/Nightmare.....50
Friend.....52
Reflections in young eyes.....53
Another day the coffee way.....55
Graveyard.....59
Penumbra Heart.....60
Snow.....61
Routine Death.....62
IMAGES.....63

Black

Some people acknowledge their mortality only at the last moment of life. The cushions that we build against death are thick and they keep its reality at bay, but sometimes the stuffing falls out through holes that are ripped open by accidents or disease. In the nursing homes, death shows its cool face at all hours of the night.

I remember one night when death had crept into the room of one older woman and seemingly caressed her face as she lay in bed. She kept getting up out of bed and coming down the hallway in her wheelchair. I remember her desperation as we kept asking her what was the matter and all she would say was "no, no, no..." After taking her back to bed, she would get back up and do it all over again. So, after a few times at this, we finally decided to tie her hands to the bed railings because we feared that she would hurt herself if she kept getting out of bed as she was weak and fragile.

After the other staff members left, I stayed in the room with the woman, sitting on a recently vacated bed next to hers. The lights were off and only a small amount of light came in from the hallway, but it was enough for me to see her twisting and turning in bed while trying to undo the restraints with her teeth. The intense silence betrayed my thoughts and I had to turn and look out the window into the black night to seek a moments refuge. The blackness seemed to flow into that small room from outside as though it were a chariot for some grim specter. She sees it as death. I see it as death too, and it is hers. For the first time she sees death and cries for escape but it is too late, for now it sits close by, like a vulture; patient and confident that it will claim its prize.

"No, no, no, I can't...", I hear her moan.

I touch her hand as a gesture of respect for I see that she will not go gentle into that good night.

Joey's Boat

I

Joseph used to have a boat,
He sailed all the time.
A sturdy craft, though somewhat small,
But still, it floated fine.

Meticulous he kept his craft,
He knew its every line.
Polished laquer all around
And every inch did shine.

Every day he'd take it out
And search about the lake.
Looking, playing, thinking, and dreaming,
All in his small wake.

Endless sun-filled afternoons and
Quiet moonless nights.
Days with water smooth as glass
Or tossed by storms delight.

Most times he would steer along,
The lines clenched in his fist.
Sometimes he'd let it steer itself
And look off in the mist.

People never understood
Although he never cared.
He found a joy in solitude
Where none could be compared.

As he became older now his
Interests slowly changed.
Almost overnight it seems his
Dreams were rearranged

"I guess I should get a job and
Maybe go to school.
Cities are the place to be
And money is the rule."

Decision made, he packed his things
And said all his good-byes,
But when he went to store his boat,
He had to dry his eyes.

As he locked it in the shed where
It would be kept dry,
He couldn't find an answer to the
Burning question; why?

II

Riding into town he felt
A dull anxiety.
He thought it was just nerves
And it should pass eventually.

But it never really did
Although he never knew,
Distracted as he was with all
The things he had to do.

The only room he could afford
Was small and old and such.
"But it will do for me" he thought
"For I don't need that much."

He found a job to pay the bills
But little more than that.
And met his first friend in the town:
A beat-up alley-cat.

Quietly he did his job
And did his best to care.
But soon he noticed curious looks
From other workers there.

He had heard the way they talked
The way they spoke in lies,
The games they played with twisted words
They wore like a disguise.

4

Beyond his understanding, it
Was not how he had learned.
And yet he felt them watching him
Everywhere he turned.

Uneasy now, he tried to talk,
To socialize and fit.
But he could never understand
Or get too close to it.

It soon began to wear on him
And then effect his mood.
He tried to act the way they did
For fear they'd think him rude.

He then began to join the guys
For evenings on the town.
Chasing girls or acting cool
Or he'd drink 'til he fell down.

Often he would sneak away
And walk back to his room
To sit alone and reminisce
Within his private tomb.

'Twas new to him, this loneliness,
Sometimes he'd sit for hours.
He'd stare outside at children playing
Or clouds or trees or flowers.

After one night with his friends
He made his way back home,
Along the streets now still and dark
Where naught but cool winds roam.

He'd drunk a bit of wine that night
His head was feeling light.
For once he felt relaxed as he
Walked on in the moonlight.

He smiled as he took a breath
Already he could tell,
That somewhere near the ocean loomed
He knew just by the smell.

Quietly he walked the trail
That slowly spiraled down
The rocky cliffs that meet the sea
Out by the edge of town.

He stopped along an old foot-bridge
That swayed a gentle motion
Above the water far below
That flowed out to the ocean.

He listened for a moment to
The rolling of the waves.
He watched the way the colors blend
And how the light behaves.

The chance to see the moonlight glow
Upon this night so fair
Could justify his loneliness
And melt off his despair.

As he stood there on that bridge
His mind was split apart
The random thoughts were drowned out by
The beating of his heart.

At the far end of the bridge
He heard a violent knock.
He looked and saw a small boat that was
Tied up to the dock.

When he moved in close to look
He then began to see
The way it moved it looked like it
Was trying to get free.

He climbed upon the dock and watched the
small boat pitch and dive.
It thrashed about so violently
As though it were alive.

Urgently he checked the ropes to
Find the knots releases
To free the little boat before it
Smashed itself to pieces.

"Get your hands off of my boat!"
A voice cried from behind.
The shock broke Josephs reverie
And brought him back to mind.

He turned and saw a man approach
And wave an angry fist.
As Joseph turned and ran his form
Was swallowed by the mist.

III

The days continued to pass on,
Each one just like the rest.
To recall any special times
Would prove to be a test!

"I think that you should find a girl"
A friend had now declared.
"You're spending too much time alone,
There's no reason to be scared."

There were some evenings on the lake
he'd watch the stars above,
And dream that somewhere watching too
Was one girl he could love.

So his consent led down a path
Where he might get a chance
To meet the girl he'd dreamt about
And wake dreams of romance.

But even this pursuit became
Another form of war.
He soon became self-conscious like
He'd never been before.

This mating game was something that
He couldn't understand.
The endless games that twist the mind
Were not what he had planned.

When it all was over and he
Just could take no more
He noticed that he only felt
More lonely than before.

IV

For ten long years he has been gone
And now he should be glad.
But on the train now homeward bound
He feels a little sad.

It seems the years had beaten him
And all he felt was numb.
He moved about as in a daze
He was blind, deaf and dumb.

Eagerly he sought the craft
He hadn't seen in years.
But when he opened up the shed
He realized his fears.

He knew neglect would have its way
With sails and chrome and wood.
But what he saw before him now
Had stopped him where he stood.

The poor boat looked so bad that Joseph
Looked away in shame
And tightly clutched the open door
When all the feelings came.

The mixture of emotions swelled
On waves of guilt and pain
When he began to fear that it
Might never sail again.

"Am I too late", he wondered now
As fear mixed in with pain
While overhead some thunder cracked
And it began to rain.

V

He went to work immediately
Deciding where to start
And spent the next days cleaning as he
Scrubbed with all his heart.

Although the boat was in bad shape
He cleaned the best he could.
He worked the places where the time
Left scars upon the wood.

The dirt came off, but left behind
A look so pale and worn.
And stitching showed where he had sewn
The sails where they were torn.

VI

Now on the lake he'd spend his days
Just laying across the bow
Staring at the water as it
Was split against the prow.

He'd been out on it several times
Since he had been back home.
He searched the coves and cliffs around
The lake he used to roam.

Days went by one after one
But something had been lost.
He'd learned a lot in ten long years
But finally, at what cost?

The passion that he used to feel
Was gone without a trace
And in its place was emptiness
And tear streaks on his face.

In his chest, a heaviness
Like chains upon his heart
Had left him feeling hopeless
And broken all apart.

He sometimes thought of suicide
When he became unsteady.
But never came to act it out
As he felt dead already.

Joseph couldn't calculate the
Years and their high toll.
He couldn't know society
Will sometimes steal your soul.

VII

It's early in the morning and
The sun has yet to rise.
But on the lake now Joseph floats
With sleep still in his eyes.

Last night the storms returned again
But now the calm prevails.
Sitting still in silence there
Is no wind for his sails.

The rhythm of the water and the
Glow the twilight cast
Left Josephs mind extended as if
Reaching for the past.

Then came a noise from somewhere near
A sound like something thrashing.
As joseph raised his weary head
He could see something splashing.

Off the starboard bow he saw an
Object up ahead.
He grabbed an oar and thrust it out
And towards the sound he sped.

He moved in close to check it out
And that was when he met
A snow white seagull caught up in
A careless hunters net.

He dropped the oar and then reached out
To stop this senseless slaughter.
But when he thought he had it made
It sank beneath the water.

Without a thought to hesitate
He jumped over the side.
But he could not see anything
No matter how he tried.

Farther down into the depths
He swam around in search
Until he felt an object brush his leg
And saw a shadow lurch

Into his view, just within reach
Of his extended hands,
He blindly grasped with fingertips
A few of the nets strands.

He grasped the bird wrapped in the net
His heart began to pound
He knew he better start back up
Or they would both be drowned.

The net cut deep into his hand
While struggling up he cursed.
He kicked his legs and swam so hard
He thought his lungs would burst.

Crashing to the top he felt the
Air flow in his chest.
Then put the bird into the boat
And climbed in with the rest.

With frantic hands he pulled the net
That tore into his skin.
He swore aloud to all the world that
This time death won't win.

And soon the net is ripped away
But now the bird lies still.
It doesn't move and Josephs fears
Are that it never will.

VIII

It's quiet now upon the lake
And all alone he stands
Looking at the shredded net
Within his bloodied hands.

He thought of murdered innocence
And as his anger swelled
He threw the net with all his strength
And as he did he yelled.

He gently took the lifeless bird
And held it to his chest.
He couldn't stop the wave of tears
Although he tried his best.

And so at last the tears flowed free
For the past and all its tolls
And Joseph cried with sympathy
For the death of two young souls.

While tears fell onto soft white down
The sun began to rise
And as the first rays touched them both
The bird opened its eyes.

While Joseph stared in disbelief
It slowly moved its head
Then slowly stood and spread it wings
While rising from the dead.

Now tears turned into laughter as he
Leaned over the boat
To scoop up some clean water and
He washed its soft white coat.

While Joseph cleaned the seagulls wings
He held it safe from harm
And sensing this the bird did rest
Its head on Joseph's arm.

The gentle bird now flapped it wings
To dry them in the sun
And Joseph watched amazed and glad
That this time life has won.

He took the bird within his arms
And held it one last time
Then gently tossed it in the air
And watched it slowly climb.

It flew in circles overhead
While farther down below
Joseph's spirit was flying too
As a breeze began to blow.

And the sun was warm upon his face
As it slowly dried the tears
And Joseph felt the joy of life
For the first time in ten years.

Chicken Nuggets

One of those strange lunches today

Drove for awhile
Ate in a parking lot somewhere
trying not to think, but failing

I would lean my head against the door post
and close my eyes and feel the soft
humid breeze on my face
and listen to the passing cars
letting the feelings wash over me

Which comes first?
   the poet or the insanity?
   the isolation or the loneliness?
   the desire or the need?

Sitting in a Volkswagen
in a parking lot
somewhere in North Dallas
I realize that I will never have
all of the answers

The Curse of the Poet

The more I talk,
the more I realize that
I don't know what I am
talking about

The more I think,
the more I think that I
am going insane

For so long
I have been trying to
find a romantic way
of explaining my insanity
in terms that will
make it seem like
an interesting and
unique way of looking at
the world

but it just won't sell

More and more often
all that I am left with
is the bare naked moment;
the hairs-breadth of time
where all is wild and beautiful
because it is untouched
by my tired human
reasoning

Hammer vs. Radio

I was working in the garage last
night

There was some music on the
radio for awhile
and then came the dreadful
commercials

I was whistling and talking out
loud to block their noise

I stopped to take a breath
when I heard the announcer
screaming "Come on, hurry and
join the crowd!"
Then another commercial came
on and I kept hearing
"Hurry, Hurry!"

I walked over to my bench and
opened one of the drawers
as the horrible commercials
spewed from the radio speaker

I reached into the drawer and
pulled out a rubber mallet
checking it against the bench a
couple of times
and feeling its balance

"Everybody's doing it!", the radio
said
"Hurry while supplies last!"

I put the mallet back into the
drawer and pulled out an axe
testing its edge with some
newspaper.

The radio continued, "Don't
be left out!, it's where America
shops!"

I put the axe down and picked
up a 10 pound sledge hammer
looking at it with a smile on my
face.

With all of my strength I hit the
radio with the hammer as it
played a commercial that had a
bastardized Beatles song in it

Pieces flew everywhere as I
pounded away on the electronic
mess

Finally satisfied
I put the hammer down gently
into the drawer

So now I sacrifice even music
for freedom

Broken

The young horse was free once
it ran wild through the hills
and across the plains
wind blowing through its mane
the thunder of its hooves echoing along the canyons
running for the pure pleasure of movement
an expression of its passionate soul
and the freedom it possessed

The man has work to do
he needs this horse
he could put it to better use, he thinks
so he captures it
and ties it down
and breaks it
and out of fear, it complies

Now its days are long
its hooves are split with nails
its back sore from its labor
and every once in a while
it looks toward the distant hills
and shakes with a vague recollection
of the freedom of its
now forgotten spirit

Teacher

Nursing a beer at the local bar,
learning the lessons of life
in this school of schools.
The things that I hear
make me more dizzy
than the beer I drink,
but it is early.

Jenny tends the bar and
is my instructor tonight
Tonight's lesson is the female
manipulation the male.
She tells me that she needs $170 for school
as she brings my beer.
She opens her little black book and finds the number of a
lawyer she knows and calls him
at home, ready to hang up if his wife answers.
He arrives about 30 minutes later and sits at the
other end of the bar.
"Watch and learn," she says with a wink.
She has his drink ready and he is impressed.
I watch her work on him and she is very good,
she has his undivided attention, the spell is cast.
After a while I ask for another beer.
As she pours, I look at her wondering if she
is having any success.
She writes "yes" on my napkin and goes
back to work.
Twenty minutes later she is folding a check for $170
and putting it in her purse as she smiles at me.
I'm impressed.
I ask her if he will expect anything in return.
"I hope not," she says and laughs.

I would have called him a fool but
there had been a moment when I wondered
where I could get $170 for her.

"Poor guy," I said.

I paid my tab and handed her a couple

of dollars for a tip telling her to buy
some pencils or something.
I could still hear her laughing as I walked out
the door.

Class was over.

Poetastry

Deep inside of me there is an
itch that I can't reach.
It bothers me,
and so you see,
I feel like I must preach.

It's not indigestion and some sex
wont ease the burn.
It is elusive,
but not exclusive,
to me, so I have learned.

Other men have argued and some
other men have written.
To those like us,
it's obvious,
by something, we've been bitten.

Preaching is a bore and I have
never done it well.
It's still a bitch,
this cosmic itch,
so I say what the hell.

Yesterday I saw something that really
made me laugh.
It did appear,
to me so clear,
just like a photograph.

A frenzied dog, in circles running,
so desperately he tried,
To no avail,
to catch his tail,
his reward was denied.

Just when he would grasp it all his
legs would trip him up.
Down he'd fall,
and there he'd sprawl,
the poor pathetic pup.

As I watched him for awhile a
new sight I did see.
His little ploy,
He did enjoy,
although quite seriously.

The endless circles that he traced
soon wore upon my mind.
Getting wound,
round and round,
I fell on my behind.

I laughed because I saw myself and
my own little game.
A different
experiment,
but futile just the same.

Pretend the thing I'm chasing is now
separate from myself,
Run around,
chase it down,
then store it on a shelf.

Time and dust collect until my
prize becomes obscure.
What once was seen,
so clear and keen,
has now become a blur.

So now I start the chase again
for truth that's crystal clear.
But now I see,
the irony,
Its always been right here.

2038

One day at a time for me
that's how I thought my life should be
always looking for the dawn
but not the day that lay beyond.
Bridges held in futures store?
I'll cross them then and not before.
Narrow had my vision grown,
A leaf unsure of where it's blown.

Innocent the numbers ran
from the pencil in my hand
calculating on a page
dates and times to guess my age.
Suddenly my writing stopped
and from my hand the pencil dropped,
my countenance expressed a grace
like water splashed into my face.
I'd stumbled on a future date,
it was the year 2 0 3 8,
and on this date the numbers told
I'd be 65 years old.
I fell back into the chair,
my eyes portrayed an empty stare,
the room no longer held my sight,
it seems my mind had taken flight.

The world of the clock had split
and I had fallen out from it.
For an instant I could see
the essence of eternity.
Time stretched out before my eyes
spacious as the summer skies,
past and future borders seen
and I was drifting in between.
Past events were plain as day.
But what I found to my dismay,
when I turned to look ahead,
everything was blank instead.
Clues were what I'd hoped to find,
but finding naught I didn't mind.
It was enough that I could climb
and walk the avenues of time.

As if sight had been restored,
potentials in my mind now roared.
So much time in front of me,
so much I have yet to see.

Back in my room with renewed sight,
inspired I began to write.
But thinking twice and feeling hearty,
I left my house and found a party.

Advice, take mine
A tribute to originality

Forget yourself, the wisemen say.
Forgetting is the only way.
Lose yourself or you may find
That you may start to lose your mind.

Know thy self, the Elders preach.
Know thy self and you can reach
Wisdom great, for its own sake.
Just don't ask how long it'll take.

Believe in God! the priests demand.
Believe or else you will be damned.
He will help you find salvation,
If you make a small donation.

Have a drink, the heathens say.
Have a smoke too, it's okay.
You start to die right at your birth,
So have fun while you're on this earth.

Fuck the world! the rebels yell.
Everyone can go to hell.
Break the rules and break the laws,
And maybe even find a cause.

Express yourself, the artists share.
Tear your jeans and grow your hair.
Then the big decision lies
In buying drugs or art supplies.

Lovers answer, sounding sure,
Love is gonna be the cure.
It will quench your dire thirst.
But you have to find it first.

Now that you have heard the rest,
Here is what I would suggest;
Take this poem and light a match.
Now hold it close so it will catch.

Put it down and watch it burn.
Watch the flames, they twist and turn.
It quickly burns and when it dies,
Watch the smoke begin to rise.

In the smoky gray-white traces,
You will start to see their faces;
People who tried to be nice,
So they gave you their advice.

They put a lock upon your mind,
And toss you in the daily grind.
Now you learn to pay the price
Of taking someones dumb advice.

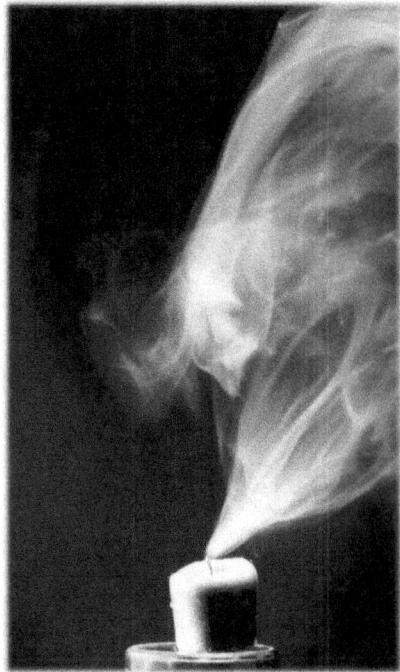

See the smoke before your eyes.
Know that words are really lies.
They can burn and block your view,
If you will allow them to.

If you're seeking something real,
There are few things words reveal.
Words can only point so far,
And then it's up to who you are.

So look and see the real joke,
When you blow away the smoke,
And clear away the ancient mess,
It's really anybodies guess.

Anna

A summer night, the air is still,
I watch the fading sky.
Sitting back to greet the night,
a memory caught my eye.

It was an evening much like this
but many years ago,
I heard the words that rang so true
from one who seemed to know.

Admitted to the nursing home,
she came under my care.
moving slow and looking tired
but with a thoughtful stare.

That night I'd helped her into bed
and wished her pleasant dreams
and was about to leave the room
to go about my schemes.

But this was when I heard a sound
and turned towards her bed.
Then I heard her say my name
and slowly lift her heard.

I stole up to the bedside now
and leaned so I could hear.
For a while she looked at me
with eyes so very clear.

She whispered that she couldn't sleep
then looked away and back.
I asked her if she wouldn't care
to join me for a snack.

She smiled and thought it wonderful
so I dismissed myself
to go and raid the kitchen
and I didn't miss a shelf.

We talked about all sorts of things,
outside the sky grew dark.
She had been a Doctor with
an office near Central Park.

Her scratchy voice took me away
and led me through her past.
Her mind took wings and I held on,
we moved along so fast.

Through the streets of old New York
we traveled with such ease,
meeting people here and there,
then passing like a breeze.

We traveled long, we traveled far,
We saw so many things.
I guess the greatest gift for some
is the joy that memory brings.

So rich in thought this woman was,
from all I heard her tell.
The currency of life is time
and she has spent hers well.

The snacks were gone, the sky was black,
the building had grown still,
the memories had stolen the time
just like they always will.

The silence hung so heavy that
it seemed the walls would burst.
I tried to find something to say
but stopped when she spoke first.

She turned and asked about myself,
her voice now soft and light.
I said I had some misplaced dreams and
I also liked to write.

She smiled and so I asked her then
if she would be so nice,
to look back through her memories
and grant me some advice.

For though I make it through the days
sometimes I'm stuck in doubt,
and she has seen so much I thought that
she might help me out.

She looked away and closed her eyes,
she seemed in total bliss.
But soon she turned her eyes on me
and said something like this;

"When you think you're different
the battle will begin,
and so it lies within your self
if you shall lose or win.

But always trust your mind my friend
for one thing you shall see,
the final test of all you hear
will be reality.

Just be yourself and do your thing,
we all need a release.
But don't forget to always keep
an eye out for the police."

We laughed and sat in silence then,
for ever is it creeping.
And soon I heard the heavy breath
that told me she was sleeping.

I looked at her and saw a life,
a life so near its end.
I thought that it was luck that I
should meet this gentle friend.

I guess it was a week or so,
I heard she passed away.
I felt as though I had been robbed
but how, I couldn't say.

No expert on the after-life,
I've crossed no astral seas,
But now I hope that when we die
we take our memories.

So once again the sky is black,
the air begins to chill.
The memories have stolen the time,
just like they always will.

Warning

There's a tornado in my soul
and it makes me lose control
within it thoughts are spinning
I am the madman grinning

So don't stand too close
for I hurt those the most
that try to look inside
at what I try to hide

There's a tornado in my soul
so violence is its toll
and that is why I say
that you should stay away

We

human

playing for love

risking it all

envy to those who win
empathy to those who lose

We

human

suffering alone

3 - 4 A.M.

alone

burning in the flames of desire

in dark rooms

in silence

privately reckoning

stretching the cord that holds us to life
stretching it until it may break

In the distance a
lone dark barks at the night
and it is *my* voice

my desperate spirit

in this desperate hour

where neither god
nor mercy
roam

If

If.
Such a small word.
And yet,
hanging from it,
suspended just
beyond my reach,
my entire future.

Teresa

She lost control and gave our eyes
A display of her mind.
And if you look behind the lies
This is what you'd find:

A little girl, anxiety,
A mass of conflicting views,
Rushing around inside her head
Paying the social dues.

No place to land inside her head,
No point to grab or hold.
No God to save her from the pain
She feels as she grows old.

She does the things we all must do
In order to survive.
But she hates them more than me or you
And wonders if she is alive.

She hates the ego she must defend,
She hates the games they play.
She only wants to be a friend
But never knows what to say.

She does her best to miss the fools,
The ones that play too hard.
They always seem to break the rules
And leave the friendship scarred.

But her job is such that she must talk
And show a degree of concern.
She fights the urge to quit and walk,
Needing money makes it burn.

She stops herself and draws a breath
Then turns and walks away.
Everytime is a little death,
Her blue sky fades to gray.

El Paso

I had to go insane last night,
it's the only way I could face,
another day on this funny rock
that's floating around in space.

The ground began to slip away
my view was slowly changed,
and when I looked around it seemed
the scene was rearranged.

The stars became like diamonds,
the sunset was orange rain,
the trees, they whispered in my ear
and the darkness called my name.

Imagination running wild,
I made the world shake.
I had the power to see in dreams
and yet I was still awake.

Control returns without request,
it's taken ungraciously.
I grin and scan the horizon
that now harbours insanity.

Imagine That

As a child in the dark
casting shadows upon the wall
the darkness was alive with monsters and maidens
demons and heroes

Before the elders convinced you that your
imagination was all in your head
it was loose in your room
under your bed
or behind the curtains

You could feel its breath on your neck
and it danced in the moonlight near the window

The elders told you that all of the dragons are dead
and all of the heroes are buried
and elves and gnomes are only in tales

Whose loss is this?

The eyes behold no magic

Natures music plays on deaf ears

What if I told you that Merlin was still around
and the sword of Kings lies waiting to be found?

What if I told you that all of the dragons have not
been killed
and the heroes graves are not yet filled?

Would you believe me?

It doesn't matter

Imagination is not something that
you believe in

It is something that you use

It is something that you are

Autumn

Once upon my course to work
I chanced upon a thread,
dangling from an orphaned tree
and down it my eye led.

It was a silken spider web
just hanging towards the ground,
and at the end the owner hung,
swinging upside down.

His legs were folded across his chest
and I moved near to peep.
So strange I thought, he seemed to be
smiling in his sleep.

How can you sleep? there's work to do,
now answer if you please!
His answer came unspoken in
a gentle autumn breeze.

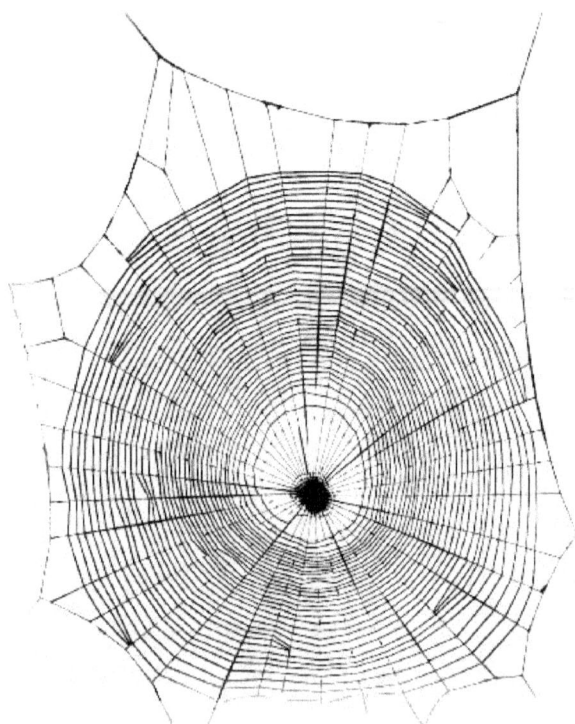

Birthday toast

The day of your birth
comes but once a year.
'Tis a day for food,
wine and a cheer.
So in honor of your birthday
we'll all fill our cup,
and try not to fall over
as we turn bottoms up.

This Mind

Give me words,
the longer the better,
like rope,
so I can tie up
this mind.
It wanders
constantly
in places it
should avoid,
like a child.

Give me words,
meaningful words,
that will
pacify it,
and control it,
because sometimes
it wont listen
and it causes trouble.

Give me words,
beautiful words,
to protect it
from all of the
ugliness in this
world.
It must not
forget what
beauty is.

Give me words,
words that rhyme,
so it can play
and make music.
In these words
it will find
its recreation
as pieces fit
like a
puzzle.

And when no words
can be found,
give me silence,
pure silence,
so it can
rest
undisturbed.

Indian Blood

Indian blood runs in
your veins.
A lovers heart pounds
in your chest.
A child's spirit glows
in your eyes.

I have seen your anger,
 carried your hate,
  endured your indifference,
   and I have felt your pain.

There are two things that can
teach a man something about
himself.
One is a small taste of death.
The other is a good woman.

I have learned so much, and
I admire you for the lessons
that you have chosen to learn
in this strange arena called
life.

Forgive my prying, animal eyes,
or be flattered.
These quick images are all that I
will ever have of you.

Forgive my silence for it is the
sadness of knowing that although
I desire all of life's experiences,
I will never know you.

Forgive this poet who hopes that
you will understand but fears that
you may not.

So Strange

So strange is life, I can't ignore,
expecting less and getting more.
I can't deny the things I seek,
I'd give so much for just one peek.
We're all the same, or so I've heard.
But some refused while some concurred.
What you choose is where you start,
the journey of the mind and heart.

I hate to think I've given up,
the classic search, the holy cup.
I guess I've found what could be found,
some things are better left unwound.

But still I ask what difference,
is in what we experience?
And if it's not in what we see,
the difference exists in me.
But now I ask if this is so,
then just how far can each one go?

Excuse me for my recreance,
before I draw my inference.

Now I know the chains that be,
are given by reality.
And doctors try to treat the brains,
that only want to break the chains.
Psyche wards, graveyards, to name but two,
are places for the ones that do.
Religion helps to ease the pull,
and make the chains more comfortable.

So peace may come to they that see,
there's one thing that will always be,
The simple truth that life is strange
is one thing that will never change.

Circle

This day is a poem, but with unspoken words.
What's usually read is now sung by the birds.
What's usually felt as a page in my hand
is the sun on my back and my toes in the sand.

Waves crashing on rocks, cool mist on my face,
gulls riding the air with Shakespearean grace.
Such beauty and magic and sparkling light.
Quick! give me a pen and some paper to write.

Silence

Like a soft blanket
I pull it up around me

Outside
those winds blow

but I am safe
for now

wrapped in silence

soothing precious
silence

massaging
ever so gently
my thoughts

Demons

Snatching at table-scraps of love

The good thing about being depressed
is that you can finally see how many
other people are depressed too

When your high horse goes lame
then you must walk like so many others

I once took my deepest emotions and gave them
to a girl when she wasn't looking.
Every time I would visit her I had to battle this demon
that I had created knowing that if I could defeat it
then I could possibly handle her,
like rescuing a princess.
On and on I'd battle, stammering and stuttering,
saying stupid things, the demon was more than
I could handle and I left each battle in pain
and shame and she would look at me strangely
as I struggled to relax because she could not see
the battle going on.
But I knew that if I won, then I could save her from
this terrible world.
After a while she realized what I had done and
decided that she didn't want my demons and she
chased the lot of us away.

So now I sit here writing while my demons
stare at me from across the room.
So you see, it's a happy ending,
for her.

The Terrible Parable

Damn, why?

Confusion and ignorance dominate
my sphere of existence

My mind is a warehouse
full of strange furniture
most of it ugly and uncomfortable
some needs to be reupholstered
as it has been worn out
and really should be thrown
away

Perhaps it is a deep-rooted
insecurity that keeps me from
letting it go
afraid that if I do, then I
will have nowhere to sit someday

Sometimes I would like to
burn it all and let the
wind have the ashes

But I fear such a fire
could get out of control

Not all of the junk in
this warehouse is mine

Some has been donated by
relatives who wanted me to
be comfortable

Off to one side is a pile
of stuff that everyone says
everyone should have
so I got mine and it is the
ugliest and most uncomfortable
of it all

I know a man who tore down
the walls of his warehouse

He says it's a little
uncomfortable at first
but very roomy

He says a person could spend
a lifetime rearranging the furniture
and all they end up with is
rearranged furniture

To be free one must
dismantle the walls

So now I have cluttered up
my warehouse with tools that
I use to try to break
down my walls

But these walls are strong
and I can only make small
chips and scratches in them

So I tell my friend
and he says that my will is
not strong enough because
it is buried under
all of the junk
"Remember" he says
"It took a long time to build
those walls, so it will take
a long time to
bring them down
In a way, you must give up everything
as in death."

So when he says that
all I can think is that
I need to sit down for
a minute.

She Sang

In the dark corner she sways.
The music pours out of the speaker
and she sways in her private shadows.
The notes, she feels them
and she absorbs them and
they run up her skin and she sings
the words and there is a tearing
as she brings the words out of her
soul and she makes them real.

Dream/Nightmare

She plays with death,
I wish I knew.
She's like a maze
I've walked into.
Her problems fit
right into mine.
I give so much,
she takes so fine.
But now my hands
are tied so tight,
I'm not sure if
it's worth the fight.
You see, I'm not sure
if she's real,
and I can't trust
the things I feel.
She acts sincere,
her family's rich.
She might be just
a spoiled bitch.
She's played me like
an instrument,
and I assumed
she was intent
on giving up
and getting out
but now I see
I've been the lout.
Self pity is her
make-up now,
that guys like me
fall for somehow.
But I should know
there's just so much
that I can do,
I'm just a crutch.
And if she can't
stand on her own,
she still must fight
her beasts alone.

But I can say,
fool that I've been,
I was sincere,
especially when,
I bared my soul
so I could reach
the thoughts that I
could use to teach.

Although it's sad,
I will endure.
But one thing still
remains unsure.
Was she my dream
with dark brown hair,
or was she just
a bad nightmare.

Friend
for Cynthia

So strange the things that fate will sometimes
throw down in my way.
I play the numbers on the dice
I toss day after day.

Within the folly of my means,
I gather up my ends.
I reach for things I wrongly think
on which my life depends.

Sometimes I find that I must stop
and run from all the strife.
That I may rest and contemplate
the meaning of my life.

But soon my thoughts begin to crowd
when I perceive the tease,
of all the questions unexplained,
and all lifes' mysteries.

At times like these I wish for one
who with these thoughts can share.
I smile and think of Cynthia,
for she is always there.

So, battle-worn and frustrated,
I come around the bend,
and trace a path unto her door,
for there I'll find a friend.

Reflections in young eyes

Mirror mirror on the wall,
before you all my secrets fall,
for I may fool everyone else,
but I could never lie to myself.

When I look into the glass,
that's when all pretensions pass.
Now I'm standing face to face,
with one more in this human race.

Do you show me all that's there?
Am I just some eyes and hair?
Or is there something I can't see,
something just too close to me?

I've heard of souls and spirits too.
And God in heaven's nothing new.
And chants and rights to set you free,
to see the world so beautifully.

I stand before tormented eyes
and laugh at such a weak disguise.
A mask I'm given when just a child,
to keep my mind from running wild.

My heart is kept from being seen,
by those who have to be so mean.
"Love just shows you're really weak.
Don't think you're really so unique."

It's a wonder we survive at all,
the way they make us weak to fall.
But now I stop between the wars,
safe behind locked mental doors.

Now safe to retrace younger days,
I climb through misty memory haze,
and there, behind the playground fence,
I find my precious innocence.

Now the mirror shows a smile.
I'll let the child be free awhile.
Excuse me while I laugh and sing,
and leave behind this suffering.

Another day the coffee way

As tired as the day is long,
try to write a decent song,
staring I am hypnotized,
much more than I realized.

Caffeine eating at my brain,
bright lights giving me eyestrain,
if my boss would disappear
I would fall asleep right here.

Looking at my watch again,
I remember way back when,
I was glad when time had passed
and five o'clock had come at last.

Now I've come to realize
just how really fast time flies,
so fast sometimes I can't say
what I did just yesterday.

Now I see time as a thief,
and I don't sigh with relief
at times passing when I'm bored,
because time can't be restored.

"Time is money" so they say.
I agree, but in a way,
it is never earned or lent,
it is really only spent.

When we're born we're very rich,
time goes by without a hitch.
Some folks fall under its spell,
Some folks try to spend it well.

Now when I look at the hour,
I am stricken by its power.
Now I see it with respect
and try to ignore its effect.

I'm not sure what costs the most,
the time we work or when we coast.
It depends on what you quest,
then you'll know what pays the best.

One more that is strange to hear
as it rings so very clear;
"cost of living's getting higher"
and were burning in its fire.

What strikes me as being funny,
it means more than spending money.
What I think is getting rough
is the time spent earning the stuff.

For those in the nine-to-five,
so that they can stay alive,
they must either get a raise,
or else they work longer days.

Now you see what is the cost;
all of the time that is lost,
working for that magic day,
retiring all old and gray.

Until then, five days a week.
Not much fun for strong or meek.
But those bills, they must be paid,
and were taught to make the grade.

Idle hands are devils tools.
I've heard this from many fools.
They're the ones who crack the whip,
we're the slaves that row the ship.

Critical? I know I am.
But I hate the traffic jam.
I see the faces in the cars,
trapped behind their hidden bars.

It may seem like I must bitch
just because I am not rich.
True, I don't have that much cash,
so my point, I will rehash.

Lets go back to where I started.
See the time that has departed.
Can I put a price on it?
Did I make it worth this writ?

Between death and my own birth,
think of what is meant by worth.
Do my values make some sense?
Are they just a vain pretense?

I don't really want to preach.
I don't even want to teach.
I only want to invest time
in my only pleasure, rhyme.

Graveyard

2:45 A.M.
Walk to the cafeteria for dinner, breakfast,
or lunch, whatever you call a meal at 2:45 A.M.
Inhale deeply a cool breeze.
Walk slow, make it last.

Pass the security guard, exchange humble greetings.

In the cafeteria, looking in the icebox, rapidly lose interest
and appetite.
Grab two little boxes of corn flakes.

Walk back a different way through the trees and their
moonlit shadows.

Pass the security guard again.
Twice is too much, something must be said.
We stop.
He says something about the trees in a weak nasal voice.
You agree and counter with a comment about the weather.
Silence,
stalemate.
I watch him closely, he wants to talk.
He continues on about the oak trees.

He must be about 65,
He smells like an ashtray, probably watches a black and white
TV all day and hides out on the graveyard shift with the
rest of us.

I have to get back so I am a murderer,
I kill the conversation.

Talk to you later.
Sure, see you later, we say with more meaning than normal.

Turn and enter the shadows.

Penumbra Heart

As hard as stones
this loners bones
the best defense?
indifference
to keep apart
this puzzle heart.

For while in pieces
it releases
the forms it holds
within its folds
and so they fly
and so can I.

And it insists
to just exist
is not enough
though it is tough
it wants to strive
to be alive.

Each moment flowing
silent knowing
my will is spent
on pure intent
to touch the light
of pure insight.

To exist is not enough
for a thing can exist
and not be alive.

Snow

I turn away from the table and the
conversation
to look out the window

It is snowing really hard
outside

I can see it against a black billboard in
the parking lot

I watch the flakes tumble passed
and am fascinated

I need nothing right now but
a few moments to watch the snow fall

This is what I want to remember
  the billowing snowflakes
  the deep gray clouds
  the slow moving traffic
  the people all bundled up slipping and
sliding on the ice
  the cool air next to the window where
I sit

These are the things that I want to
remember

Not the bad joke that a guy at the table
just told
nor the pointers on interest rates and
bank funds that I
was just informed of

I want to remember how I thought of a
girl I know
as I watched the snow coming down and
blowing
across the frozen grass

Routine Death

One of those days
where everything seems so stupid.

The long line of cars
all on the death-march to work,
it seems so damn stupid
that I can barely summon the
energy to shift into the next gear.

The voices on the radio,
normally irritating anyway,
are particularly disgusting today;
I turned it off
a few miles back.

I think of my boss,
and my bosses boss,
and all of the meaningless pursuits
of the forthcoming day
and I want to pull off the road
and walk out into the field
and just sit in the grass.
But reactions like this
have been bred out of me
and I roll on.

And as I sit at my stupid desk
with my stupid cup
filled with stupid coffee
listening to all of the stupid voices,
my mind wanders back to that field
where the grass almost seemed to not be stupid.

IMAGES

I

I've been there yes, I've seen the place,
It's etched in lines upon my face.
Its sights and sounds forever grind
Upon the machine of my mind.

The bitter smell, the faded light,
The muffled cries throughout the night;
Despondent humans safely stored,
From danger in that sad psyche ward.

The hallways stretch so far it seems
They reach into my darkest dreams.
Behind the doors that line each side,
The specters from my nightmares hide.

I've walked the hallways countless times,
While up my back a shiver climbs.
And even now as I reflect,
I never know what to expect...

II

Today it's quiet as I roam
This institution some call home,
With people passing different ways,
Wrapped in their medicated daze.

And now I see the doctors prowl.
I know them by their bitter scowl.
Now passing quickly out of sight,
Within their doctors' coats of white.

Across the hall, Ms. Janet Keyes
Is helped along by orderlies.
They walk her to a corner door,
Just like so many times before.

They go inside and out of view,
But I know some of what they do.
They lay her down and give her shots,
And bind her hands with leather knots.

Then throw a switch; one hundred volts,
To clear her mind with violent jolts.
Her body twists in spasms then,
As it is held down by the men.

Within that moment, taut and grim,
I fancy that the lights grow dim.
And for a moment cross the line
To see the lab of Frankenstein.

I wonder at how much they know,
And how far they have yet to go.
I think for all their fatal flaws,
They treat the symptoms, not the cause.

They let her up and say she's cured,
But I know now that it's absurd.
By looking closer I can see
It's all just electricity.

III

I knew the man in room 12A
Who finally snapped one summer day.
I watched his violent reverie,
But there was so much more to see.

I think it was his finest hour.
He'd finally tapped an unused power.
His speech at once became intense,
Charged with a violent eloquence.

64

And as he went, he quickly bore
Upon this latent reservoir.
With all our eyes on him he spoke
Of how this world was such a joke.

"All shame's on us, this human race,
To see our doom but turn our face.
You must be blind if you can't see,
It happens all through history.

We think we're free, but look around,
And see that we are safely bound,
By so-called leaders pulling strings,
The freedom bell no longer rings.

They say that it's for our own good
That they must steal our livelihood,
Manipulate us with their tools,
While we just sit and watch like fools."

Then like a beast within a cage,
He had an instant surge of rage.
He stopped just momentarily,
And threw a chair at the TV.

A perfect shot, his aim was right,
And much to all of our delight,
We watched it spark and smoke and burn,
And so the story took a turn.

And now he smiled and took a breath,
Prepared to take on even death.
He raised his hands into the air
And spoke to us in mock despair.

"Alas my friends, you hesitate,
As if you know that it's too late.
Well I can tell by your behavior
That you're still waiting for your saviour."

By now a force grew by the door,
A sturdy crew of six or more,
Equipped with straps and sheets and such;
The tools for those who talk too much.

He turned and saw them moving in.
Aware his time was wearing thin,
He spoke now in a furtive way,
The last words he would ever say.

"My friends I leave to you this war,
For I can't fight it anymore.
There's only one place left to try,
And there I'll go or else I'll die.

So stay alert and keep an eye
On all these liars while they try
To sneak around where you are blind,
And try to reprogram your mind."

They grabbed him and they took him down.
He cried his tears as he was bound.
And with one final look at me,
He broke the link and he was free.

His eyes took on an empty stare.
They focused neither here nor there.
But somewhere else, I couldn't see,
Somewhere beyond reality.

A smile played across his face,
Then went away and left no trace.
And then his countenance was blank.
His body froze and then it sank.

He's strapped in bed ironically,
For all he wants is to be free.
But now I look and see his hands
Are wrapped in padded leather bands.

So now he lies devoid of feeling,
Just staring blindly at the ceiling.
His muscles pinch and bind like knots,
Meanwhile his body slowly rots.

I ask myself why he'd decide
To run this mental suicide.
But I don't have that far to go;
I think that many people know.

Is this the fate of those who see
Beyond our dark reality,
Or was he simply paranoid,
And thus his vision was destroyed?

IV

Melissa's been here three months now.
She's like a ghost that knows just how
To haunt me with her mystery
Of being here but hard to see.

Like all the others she was there
Because she simply didn't care.
A pretty girl, like crystal; clear,
Just touch her and she'd disappear.

And as I look upon her face,
I'm stricken by its gentle grace.
I trace its lines with cautious eyes,
For fear that she may realize.

My interest might be taken wrong,
So I dare not come on too strong.
But orbit her just within sight;
A distant silent satellite.

We passed some moments quietly.
We'd sit alone, just her and me.
Look through the glass across the way,
At what the fates might show that day.

"The birds are great" I hear her say.
She wishes she could fly away.
She points towards her one delight;
A graceful dove of unstained white.

And as she points her hand it twists
To show the scars upon her wrists.
The marks are there but who can know
How deep the scars can truly go.

A victim of her father's lust,
He broke that simple sacred trust.
And though he was the evil first,
It seems that he was not the worst.

It's sad for he was just the start,
As soon came others who took part.
They've stolen what was never theirs,
That vile cast of characters.

So now I see her innocence
Is burdened with this black offense.
I see it weigh upon her soul,
And fear it soon may take its toll.

The night was made for girls like this,
A landscape soft with sable bliss.
They wander in its privacy,
A haven from reality.

For here they dream, if they should dare,
Of someone who might someday care.
Or meet their demons for the fight,
And battle on throughout the night.

The final test lies buried deep
Beyond the misty wall of sleep,
Where if they find that they can't cope,
They end it all with pills or rope.

Within the flow of death's release
They walk the smooth terrain of peace,
Where they can let the pain unfurl.
And so it was with this poor girl.

One morning when they checked her bed
Was when they found that she was dead.
She took what little life remained
And left before it could be drained.

I sit alone since she is gone
And watch the birds out on the lawn.
I search for thoughts in vain to find
Her empty chair reflects my mind.

Each time they go, they take a part,
And leave a hole inside my heart.
I laugh because I must concede
If it weren't empty, it would bleed.

V

It's quiet now, the day is done.
I watch the pastel setting sun
As shadows grow against the walls
And start to roam along the halls.

I sometimes try to summarize
The evidence before my eyes.
To bring it forth in present tense
To see if it might make some sense.

Now after all the years have passed,
I gather all the facts at last,
And when I look I now can see
A model of society.

Each patient represents a group
Extracted from the social soup,
And placed within those guarded walls
Where all they hear are doctors calls.

Since now their movements are contained,
Then maybe they can be explained.
Now scaled down, they slowly pass
Beneath the doctors looking glass.

The doctor's judgments are then based
On social laws that have been placed
By those who think they know what's sane
But how they know, they won't explain.

So if we choose to walk a trail
That keeps us from this mental jail,
Then all we really have to know
Is how to act the Status Quo.

How long can one who goes his way
Avoid this trap that grows each day?
You might be careful where you tread,
Lest they should get inside your head.

So now I peek between the cracks
And try to bind the bitter facts,
To peer straight at society,
And archive its new legacy.

But all that's stored upon the shelf
Is what it's doing to itself,
How it tries to hide the truth,
And rape the innocence of youth.